Mail Trucks

Julie Murray

Abdo
MY COMMUNITY: VEHICLES
Kids

abdopublishing.com

Published by Abdo Kids, a division of ABDO, PO Box 398166, Minneapolis, Minnesota 55439.
Copyright © 2016 by Abdo Consulting Group, Inc. International copyrights reserved in all countries.
No part of this book may be reproduced in any form without written permission from the publisher.

Printed in the United States of America, North Mankato, Minnesota.

102015

012016

Photo Credits: Alamy, Corbis, iStock, Shutterstock, ©Tupungato p.7, ©Julie Clopper p.21,
©Greg K_ca p.22, ©Leonard Zhukovsky p.22,23 / Shutterstock.com

Production Contributors: Teddy Borth, Jennie Forsberg, Grace Hansen

Design Contributors: Candice Keimig, Dorothy Toth

Library of Congress Control Number: 2015941775

Cataloging-in-Publication Data

Murray, Julie.
 Mail trucks / Julie Murray.
  p. cm. -- (My community: vehicles)
ISBN 978-1-68080-131-6

Includes index.

1. Postal service--United States--Transportation, Automotive--Juvenile literature. I. Title.

629.223--dc23

                    2015941775

Table of Contents

Mail Truck

Mara waits for the mail.

Here comes the mail truck!

The truck is white. It has a blue stripe. It has a red stripe, too.

We Deliver For You.

www.usps.com

CVS/pharmacy

10704

7

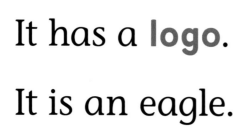

It has a **logo**.

It is an eagle.

www.usps.com

www.usps.com

A mail carrier drives the truck.

She brings the mail.

www.usps.com

UNITED STATES
POSTAL SERVICE

11

The steering wheel is on the right. She can reach the mailbox.

The mail is kept in the back.

It is **organized**.

15

The truck **collects** the mail, too. It takes it to the post office.

Mail trucks run six days a week. No mail on Sunday!

Have you seen a mail truck?

www.usps.com

Parts of a Mail Truck

lights

steering wheel

logo

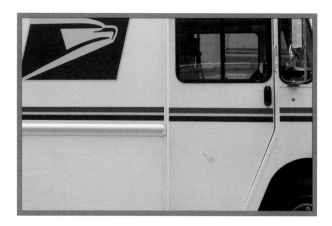

stripes

Glossary

collect
to bring together.

logo
a symbol or design that represents
an organization.

organized
arranged in a certain way.

Index

abdokids.com

Use this code to log on to abdokids.com and access crafts, games, videos, and more!

Abdo Kids Code:
MMK1316